interchange

FIFTH EDITION

1B

Workbook

Jack C. Richards

with Jonathan Hull and Susan Proctor

CAMBRIDGE
UNIVERSITY PRESS

Shaftesbury Road, Cambridge CB2 8EA, United Kingdom

One Liberty Plaza, 20th Floor, New York, NY 10006, USA

477 Williamstown Road, Port Melbourne, VIC 3207, Australia

314–321, 3rd Floor, Plot 3, Splendor Forum, Jasola District Centre, New Delhi – 110025, India

103 Penang Road, #05-06/07, Visioncrest Commercial, Singapore 238467

Cambridge University Press & Assessment is a department of the University of Cambridge.

We share the University's mission to contribute to society through the pursuit of
education, learning and research at the highest international levels of excellence.

www.cambridge.org
Information on this title: www.cambridge.org/9781316622667

© Cambridge University Press & Assessment 1990, 1997, 2005, 2013, 2017

First published 1990
Second edition 1997
Third edition 2005
Fourth edition 2013
Fifth edition 2017
Fifth edition update published 2021

20 19 18 17 16 15 14 13 12 11 10 9 8 7

Printed in Great Britain by Ashford Colour Press Ltd.

A catalogue record for this publication is available from the British Library.

ISBN 978-1-009-04044-0 Student's Book 1 with eBook
ISBN 978-1-009-04047-1 Student's Book 1A with eBook
ISBN 978-1-009-04048-8 Student's Book 1B with eBook
ISBN 978-1-009-04063-1 Student's Book 1 with Digital Pack
ISBN 978-1-009-04064-8 Student's Book 1A with Digital Pack
ISBN 978-1-009-04065-5 Student's Book 1B with Digital Pack
ISBN 978-1-316-62247-6 Workbook 1
ISBN 978-1-316-62254-4 Workbook 1A
ISBN 978-1-316-62266-7 Workbook 1B
ISBN 978-1-108-40606-2 Teacher's Edition 1
ISBN 978-1-316-62226-1 Class Audio 1
ISBN 978-1-009-04066-2 Full Contact 1 with Digital Pack
ISBN 978-1-009-04067-9 Full Contact 1A with Digital Pack
ISBN 978-1-009-04068-6 Full Contact 1B with Digital Pack
ISBN 978-1-108-40306-1 Presentation Plus 1

Additional resources for this publication at cambridgeone.org

Contents

Credits

Illustrations

Pablo Gallego (Beehive Illustration): 42, 53, 65, 78, 91; **Thomas Girard** (Good Illustration): 3, 25, 50, 72, 92; **Quino Marin** (The Organisation): 2, 47, 54, 66; **Gavin Reece** (New Division): 15, 48, 52(B); **Paul Williams** (Sylvie Poggio Artists): 51.

Photos

Back cover (woman with whiteboard): Jenny Acheson/Stockbyte/GettyImages; Back cover (whiteboard): Nemida/GettyImages; Back cover (man using phone): Betsie Van Der Meer/Taxi/GettyImages; Back cover (woman smiling): PeopleImages.com/DigitalVision/GettyImages; Back cover (name tag): Tetra Images/GettyImages; Back cover (handshake): David Lees/Taxi/GettyImages; p. 1: Jon Feingersh/Blend Images/Brand X Pictures/GettyImages; p. 4 (TL): Juanmonino/iStock/GettyImages Plus/GettyImages; p. 4 (BL): Caiaimage/Chris Ryan/OJO+/GettyImages; p. 4 (TR): XiXinXing/GettyImages; p. 4 (BR): powerofforever/E+/GettyImages; p. 5: PeopleImages/DigitalVision/GettyImages; p. 6: Martin Barraud/Caiaimage/GettyImages; p. 7 (photo 1): Jetta Productions/Blend Images/GettyImages; p. 7 (photo 2): Oleksandr Rupeta/NurPhoto/GettyImages; p. 7 (photo 3): Hill Street Studios/Blend Images/GettyImages; p. 7 (photo 4): Jupiterimages/Photolibrary/GettyImages; p. 8: Monty Rakusen/Cultura/GettyImages; p. 9: Matt Hage/Design Pics/First Light/GettyImages; p. 10 (TL): Digital Vision/DigitalVision/GettyImages; p. 10 (TR): Hybrid Images/Cultura/GettyImages; p. 10 (BR): kali9/E+/GettyImages; p. 11: kali9/E+/GettyImages; p. 12 (T): Hybrid Images/Cultura/GettyImages; p. 12 (BL): Visage/Stockbyte/GettyImages; p. 12 (BC): segawa7/iStock/GettyImages Plus/GettyImages; p. 12 (BR): asterix0597/E+/GettyImages; p. 13: Westend61/GettyImages; p. 14: Robert Niedring/Alloy/GettyImages; p. 16 (silver earrings): JohnGollop/iStock/GettyImages Plus/GettyImages; p. 16 (gold earrings): cobalt/iStock/GettyImages Plus/GettyImages; p. 16 (leather coat): bonetta/iStock/GettyImages Plus/GettyImages; p. 16 (wool coat): DonNichols/E+/GettyImages; p. 16 (orange shirt): rolleiflextlr/iStock/GettyImages Plus/GettyImages; p. 16 (gray shirt): popovaphoto/iStock/GettyImages Plus/GettyImages; p. 16 (cotton dresses): Evgenii Karamyshev/Hemera/GettyImages Plus/GettyImages; p. 16 (silk dresses): Paolo_Toffanin/iStock/GettyImages Plus/GettyImages; p. 17 (gold ring): Image Source/GettyImages; p. 17 (silver ring): ProArtWork/E+/GettyImages; p. 17 (tablet): luismmolina/E+/GettyImages; p. 17 (laptop computer): Howard Kingsnorth/The Image Bank/GettyImages; p. 17 (hiking boots): AlexRaths/iStock/GettyImages Plus/GettyImages; p. 17 (sneakers): badmanproduction/iStock/GettyImages Plus/GettyImages; p. 17 (wool gloves): popovaphoto/iStock/GettyImages Plus/GettyImages; p. 17 (leather gloves): Hugh Threlfall/Stockbyte/GettyImages; p. 17 (black sunglasses): Vladimir Liverts/Hemera/GettyImages Plus/GettyImages; p. 17 (white sunglasses): Dimedrol68/iStock/GettyImages Plus/GettyImages; p. 18 (photo 3): csfotoimages/iStock/GettyImages Plus/GettyImages; p. 18 (photo 1): Donald Iain Smith/Moment/GettyImages; p. 18 (photo 4): goir/iStock/GettyImages Plus/GettyImages; p. 18 (photo 2): Marc Romanelli/Blend Images/GettyImages; p. 19 (T): Larry Busacca/GettyImages Entertainment/GettyImages North America/GettyImages; p. 19 (B): Steve Granitz/WireImage/GettyImages; p. 20 (photo 1): Brian Bahr/GettyImages North America/GettyImages; p. 20 (photo 2): Phillip Faraone/GettyImages North America/GettyImages; p. 20 (photo 3): Anthony Harvey/GettyImages Entertainment/GettyImages Europe/GettyImages; p. 20 (photo 4): Taylor Hill/FilmMagic/GettyImages; p. 20 (BR): Jon Kopaloff/FilmMagic/GettyImages; p. 21 (R): DianaHirsch/E+/GettyImages; p. 21 (L): ILM/Universal Studios/GettyImages; p. 23 (T): Shirlaine Forrest/WireImage/GettyImages; p. 23 (B): Moof/Cultura/GettyImages; p. 24 (T): Mike Windle/GettyImages Entertainment/GettyImagesNorth America/GettyImages; p. 24 (B): Donald Miralle/DigitalVision/GettyImages; p. 26: Copyright Anek/Moment/GettyImages; p. 27 (photo 1): Echo/Cultura/GettyImages; p. 27 (photo 2): Juice Images/Cultura/GettyImages; p. 27 (photo 3): Christopher Hope-Fitch/Moment/GettyImages; p. 27 (photo 4): sjenner13/iStock/GettyImages Plus/GettyImages; p. 27 (photo 5): Hero Images/GettyImages; p. 30 (L): Soumen Nath Photography/Moment Open/GettyImages; p. 30 (R): Chaos/The Image Bank/GettyImages; p. 31 (L): Tetra Images/GettyImages; p. 31 (R): John Freeman/Dorling Kindersley/GettyImages; p. 33 (T): Westend61/GettyImages; p. 33 (B): Adam Gault/Photodisc/GettyImages; p. 34 (T): Camilla Watson/AWL Images/GettyImages; p. 34 (C): Stephen McCarthy/Sportsfile/GettyImages; p. 34 (B): PhotoAlto/Laurence Mouton/PhotoAlto Agency RF Collections/GettyImages; p. 35: Koji Aoki/Aflo/GettyImages; p. 36: PeopleImages/DigitalVision/GettyImages; p. 37: Jan Speiser/EyeEm/GettyImages; p. 38 (L): PeopleImages/DigitalVision/GettyImages; p. 38 (R): asiseeit/E+/GettyImages; p. 40 (T): PRASIT CHANSAREEKORN/Moment/GettyImages; p. 40 (B): Tuul and Bruno Morandi/Photolibrary/GettyImages; p. 41 (T): Boy_Anupong/Moment/GettyImages; p. 41 (B): John W Banagan/Lonely Planet Images/GettyImages; p. 46 (L): Allison Michael Orenstein/The Image Bank/GettyImages; p. 46 (R): Plume Creative/DigitalVision/GettyImages; p. 49: Jim Franco/Taxi/GettyImages; p. 52 (boots): StockPhotosArt/iStock/GettyImages Plus/GettyImages; p. 52 (cap): ljpat/E+/GettyImages; p. 52 (dress): pidjoe/E+/GettyImages; p. 52 (high heels): LOVE_LIFE/iStock/GettyImages Plus/GettyImages; p. 52 (jeans): gofotograf/iStock/GettyImages Plus/GettyImages; p. 52 (jewelry): DEA/L. DOUGLAS/De Agostini Editorial/GettyImages; p. 52 (necktie): Wilshireimages/E+/GettyImages; p. 52 (shirt): Alex Cao/Photodisc/GettyImages; p. 52 (shorts): stocksnapper/iStock/GettyImages Plus/GettyImages; p. 52 (sneakers): Tevarak/iStock/GettyImages Plus/GettyImages;

p. 52 (suit): bonetta/iStock/GettyImages Plus/GettyImages; p. 52 (T-shirt): GaryAlvis/E+/GettyImages; p. 55 (T): Blake Little/Stone/GettyImages; p. 55 (C): Jenner Images/Moment Open/GettyImages; p. 55 (B): Kevin Kozicki/Image Source/GettyImages; p. 56: Barry Austin Photography/Iconica/GettyImages; p. 57 (photo 1): sutichak/iStock/GettyImages Plus/GettyImages; p. 57 (photo 2): Koichi Kamoshida/Photolibrary/GettyImages; p. 57 (photo 3): Westend61/GettyImages; p. 57 (photo 4): Paul Bradbury/OJO Images/GettyImages; p. 57 (photo 5): Jan Hetfleisch/GettyImages Europe/GettyImages; p. 57 (photo 6): Halfdark/GettyImages; p. 58 (T): Jupiterimages/Photos.com/GettyImages Plus/GettyImages; p. 58 (B): Nmaverick/iStock/GettyImages Plus/GettyImages; p. 59 (text messaging): skynesher/E+/GettyImages; p. 59 (rugby match): Stewart Cohen/Photolibrary/GettyImages; p. 59 (sushi): Steve Brown Photography/Photolibrary/GettyImages; p. 59 (houston): Gavin Hellier/Photographer's Choice/GettyImages; p. 60: Sam Edwards/Caiaimage/GettyImages; p. 61 (L): Martin Puddy/Stone/GettyImages; p. 61 (R): Karina Wang/Photographer's Choice/GettyImages; p. 62 (L): jimkruger/iStock/GettyImages Plus/GettyImages; p. 62 (C): AzmanL/iStock/GettyImages Plus/GettyImages; p. 62 (R): Jonas Gratzer/LightRocket/GettyImages; p. 63 (T): Alberto Manuel Urosa Toledano/Moment/GettyImages; p. 63 (B): DUCEPT Pascal/hemis.fr/GettyImages; p. 64 (BL): Sungjin Kim/Moment Open/GettyImages; p. 64 (TC): RODRIGO BUENDIA/AFP/GettyImages; p. 64 (BR): Andrea Pistolesi/Photolibrary/GettyImages; p. 65: JTB/UIG/GettyImages; p. 68: BSIP/UIG/GettyImages; p. 69: KidStock/Blend Images/GettyImages; p. 70: YinYang/E+/GettyImages; p. 71: Ariel Skelley/Blend Images/GettyImages; p. 73 (photo 1): Peter Dazeley/Photographer's Choice/GettyImages; p. 73 (photo 2): whitewish/E+/GettyImages; p. 73 (photo 3): Chuck Kahn/EyeEm/GettyImages; p. 73 (photo 4): lisafx/iStock/GettyImages Plus/GettyImages; p. 73 (photo 5): TUGIO MURATA/amanaimagesRF/GettyImages; p. 73 (photo 6): Creative Crop/DigitalVision/GettyImages; p. 74 (greasy): David Crunelle/EyeEm/GettyImages; p. 74 (bland): Howard Shooter/GettyImages; p. 74 (rich): Johner Images/GettyImages; p. 74 (salty): Creativ Studio Heinemann/GettyImages; p. 74 (healthy): Verdina Anna/Moment/GettyImages; p. 75 (Carlota): andresr/E+/GettyImages; p. 75 (Luka): NicolasMcComber/E+/GettyImages; p. 75 (Adam): David Harrigan/Canopy/GettyImages; p. 76 (broccoli): Kevin Summers/Photographer's Choice/GettyImages; p. 76 (sushi): Food Image Source/StockFood Creative/GettyImages; p. 76 (cream cone): dlerick/E+/GettyImages; p. 77: gchutka/E+/GettyImages; p. 79 (T): Richard Roscoe/Stocktrek Images/GettyImages; p. 79 (C): www.sierralara.com/Moment/GettyImages; p. 79 (B): Yevgen Timashov/Cultura/GettyImages; p. 80: Ulf Andersen/GettyImages Europe/GettyImages; p. 81 (Badwater Basin): David ToussaintMoment/GettyImages; p. 81 (Suez Canal): Jacques Marais/Gallo Images/GettyImages; p. 81 (Mount Waialeale): M Swiet Productions/Moment Open/GettyImages; p. 82: Christian Vorhofer/imageBROKER/GettyImages; p. 83 (Angel Falls): Jane Sweeney/AWL Images/GettyImages; p. 83 (Yangtze River): View Stock/GettyImages; p. 83 (Antarctica): Michael Nolan/robertharding/GettyImages; p. 83 (Rain forest): JohnnyLye/iStock/GettyImages Plus/GettyImages; p. 83 (Grand Canyon): Stephanie Hohmann/EyeEm/GettyImages; p. 84: GlobalP/iStock/GettyImages Plus/GettyImages; p. 86: Emilio Cobos/Euroleague Basketball/GettyImages; p. 87 (go to park): Feverpitched/iStock/GettyImages Plus/GettyImages; p. 87 (go to concerts): Yuri_Arcurs/DigitalVision/GettyImages; p. 87 (have parties): SolStock/E+/GettyImages; p. 87 (see plays): VisitBritain/Eric Nathan/Britain On View/GettyImages; p. 87 (watch horror movies): Crazytang/E+/GettyImages; p. 87 (go on picnics): Kentaroo Tryman/Maskot/GettyImages; p. 88 (Hannah): Dianne Avery Photography/GettyImages; p. 88 (Pablo): Jacqueline Veissid/Blend Images/GettyImages; p. 88 (Richard): Laura Doss/Image Source/GettyImages; p. 88 (Lien): iPandastudio/iStock/GettyImages Plus/GettyImages; p. 88 (Kalil): Juanmonino/E+/GettyImages; p. 88 (Rachel): Westend61/GettyImages; p. 88 (Eliana): billnoll/E+/GettyImages; p. 88 (Daichi): petekarici/iStock/GettyImages Plus/GettyImages; p. 90: ichaka/E+/GettyImages; p. 93 (L): Paul Bradbury/Caiaimage/GettyImages; p. 93 (TR): Hero Images/GettyImages; p. 93 (CR): Hero Images/DigitalVision/GettyImages; p. 94: Zero Creatives/Cultura/GettyImages; p. 95 (T): DragonImages/iStock/GettyImages Plus/GettyImages; p. 95 (C): agentry/iStock/GettyImages Plus/GettyImages; p. 95 (B): Digital Vision/Photodisc/GettyImages; p. 96: Deb Snelson/Moment/GettyImages.

9 What does she look like?

1 Write the opposites. Use the words in the box.

☑ light   ☐ straight   ☐ young   ☐ short   ☐ tall

1. dark / _____light_____

2. curly / _____

3. short / _____

4. long / _____

5. elderly / _____

2 Descriptions

A Match the words in columns A and B. Write the descriptions.

A	B		
☑ medium	☐ aged	**1.**	medium height
☐ fairly	☐ brown	**2.**	
☐ good	☑ height	**3.**	
☐ middle	☐ long	**4.**	
☐ dark	☐ looking	**5.**	

B Answer the questions using the descriptions from part A.

1. A: How tall is he?

   B: _He's medium height._

2. A: What does he look like?

   B: _____

3. A: What color is his hair?

   B: _____

4. A: How long is his hair?

   B: _____

5. A: How old is he?

   B: _____

3 Complete this conversation with questions.

Marta: Let's find Arturo. I need to talk to him.

Alli: _What does he look like?_

Marta: He's very handsome, with curly brown hair.

Alli: And _____

Marta: It's medium length.

Alli: _____

Marta: He's fairly tall.

Alli: And _____

Marta: He's in his early twenties.

Alli: _____

Marta: Well, he usually wears jeans.

Alli: I think I see him over there. Is that him?

4 Describe yourself. How old are you? What do you look like? What are you wearing today?

_____
_____
_____
_____
_____

5 **Circle two things in each description that do not match the picture. Then correct the information.**

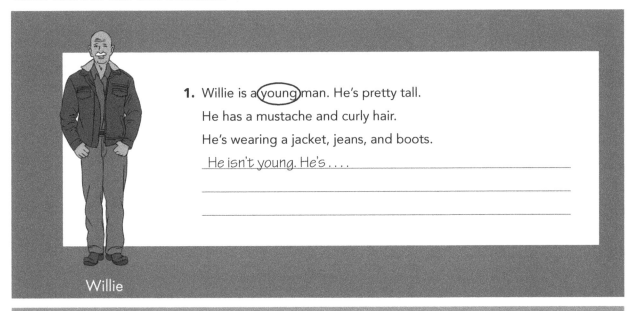

1. Willie is a (young) man. He's pretty tall.
   He has a mustache and curly hair.
   He's wearing a jacket, jeans, and boots.

   He isn't young. He's . . . .

   _____

   _____

Willie

2. Sandy is about 25. She's very pretty.
   She's medium height. Her hair is long and blond.
   She's wearing a black sweater, a skirt, and sneakers.

   _____

   _____

   _____

Sandy

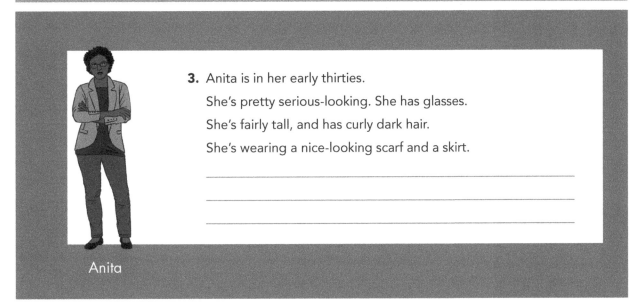

3. Anita is in her early thirties.
   She's pretty serious-looking. She has glasses.
   She's fairly tall, and has curly dark hair.
   She's wearing a nice-looking scarf and a skirt.

   _____

   _____

   _____

Anita

6 Which of these clothing items are more formal? Which are more casual?
Complete the chart.

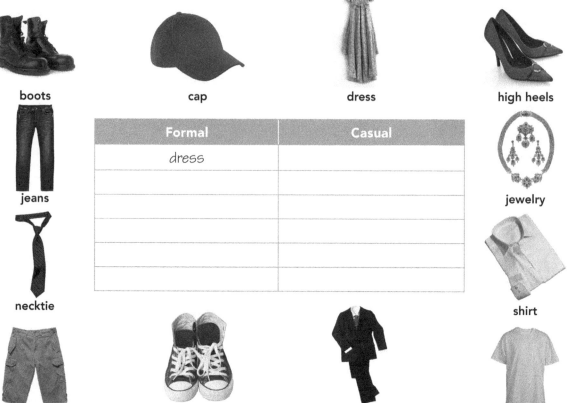

boots

cap

dress

high heels

jeans

Formal	Casual
dress	

jewelry

necktie

shirt

shorts

sneakers

suit

T-shirt

7 Write a sentence about the people in the picture. Use the words in the box
and participles.

☑ man	☐ carry a jacket
☐ one	☐ wear sunglasses
☐ ones	☑ stand next to Angela
☐ short man	☐ talk to the man
☐ young woman	☐ wear a suit and tie

1. <u>Brad is the man standing next to Angela.</u>
2. _____
3. _____
4. _____
5. _____

Brad   Angela   Li Na   Matt   Tiffany   Rodrigo

8 Write sentences about the people in the picture. Use the words given.

1. _Charles and Natalie are the ones playing chess._ (ones / playing chess)
2. _____ (one / behind the couch)
3. _____ (ones / eating pizza)
4. _____ (woman / on the couch)
5. _____ (man / short black hair)

9 Rewrite the conversations. Find another way to say the sentences using the words in the box.

☑ near ☐ sitting ☐ wearing ☑ which ☐ who ☐ who

1. **A:** Who's Lucas?

   Which one's Lucas?

   B: He's the guy next to the window.

   He's the guy near the window.

2. **A:** Which ones are the servers?

   _____

   B: They're the ones in the red polo shirts.

   _____

3. **A:** Which one is Naomi?

   _____

   B: She's the one on the couch next to Lisa.

   _____

10 Which one is Jeff?

Complete Bill and Ruby's conversation at a party. Use the present continuous or the participle of the verbs in the box.

☐ cook ☐ eat ☑ look ☐ play ☐ sit ☐ talk ☐ use ☐ wear

Ruby: I'm glad you brought me to this party, Bill. I'm _____ looking _____ for someone here named Jeff.

Bill: Yeah, I don't know too many people here. But let's try to find him. Is he one of those guys _____ football? What about the guy with black hair and _____ the dark T-shirt?

Ruby: Hmm, no. That's not Jeff.

Bill: How about the one _____ the music system over there, in the white T-shirt.

Ruby: No, I know him. That's Ken.

Bill: Hmm. Oh, is that Jeff _____ at the table and _____ to the two women? It looks like they're already _____.

Ruby: No, not him, either. Gee, I wonder if Jeff even came to the party?

Bill: Well, he can't be the chef, right? The guy _____ vegetables at the grill?

Ruby: That's him! Hey, Jeff!

11 Choose the correct responses.

1. A: Who's Shawn?

   B: _The middle-aged man on the couch._
   - The middle-aged man on the couch.
   - That's right.

2. A: Where's Samantha?

   B: _____
   - She couldn't make it.
   - I'd like to meet her.

3. A: Is Avery the one wearing glasses?

   B: _____
   - That's right.
   - She's running late.

4. A: How tall is she?

   B: _____
   - Fairly long.
   - Pretty short.

10 Have you ever been there?

1 Match the verb forms in columns A and B.

A	B
1. make __g__	a. tried
2. ride _____	b. eaten
3. do _____	c. seen
4. eat _____	d. had
5. go _____	e. ridden
6. have _____	f. heard
7. be _____	✓ g. made
8. hear _____	h. done
9. see _____	i. gone
10. try _____	j. been

2 Complete the questions in these conversations. Use the present perfect of the verbs in Exercise 1.

1. A: _____Have you seen_____ Al's new dog?

   B: Yes, it's so cute!

2. A: How many times _____
   to the gym this month?

   B: Actually, not at all. Let's go later today!

3. A: How many phone calls _____
   today?

   B: I made two calls – both to you!

4. A: _____ your homework yet?

   B: Yes, I have. I did it after class.

5. A: _____ at the new Italian
   restaurant?

   B: Yes, we already have. It's very good but a
   little expensive.

6. A: How long _____
   those boots?

   B: I bought them on Monday.

3 *Already* and *yet*

A Check (✓) the things you've already done. Put an ✗ next to the things you haven't done yet.

1. _____ graduated from high school
2. _____ gotten married
3. _____ ridden a horse
4. _____ been in an airplane
5. _____ learned to drive
6. _____ traveled abroad

B Write sentences about each activity in part A. Use *already* and *yet*.

> **Grammar note: *Already* and *yet***
>
> ***Already* is used in positive statements with the present perfect.**
> I've **already** graduated from high school.
>
> ***Yet* is used in negative statements with the present perfect.**
> I haven't gotten married **yet**.

1. _____
   _____
2. _____
   _____
3. _____
   _____
4. _____
   _____
5. _____
   _____
6. _____
   _____

4 Complete these sentences with *for* or *since*.

1. Jill has driven the same car ___since___ 2004.
2. I have been a teacher _____ several years.
3. I haven't had this much fun _____ I was a kid!
4. I'm so sleepy. I've been awake _____ 4:00 this morning.
5. Kyoko was an exchange student in Peru _____ a whole semester.
6. Marcus has lived in Dubai _____ 2010.
7. How are you? I haven't seen you _____ high school.
8. Where have you been? I've been here _____ over an hour!
9. Mr. and Mrs. Lopez have been married _____ nearly 50 years.

5 Look at these pictures. How often have you done these things? Write sentences using the expressions in the box.

I've . . . many times.	I've . . . once or twice.
I've . . . three or four times.	I haven't . . . lately.
I've . . . several times.	I've never . . .

eat Thai food

go to a concert

1. _____

2. _____

go skiing

play an instrument

3. _____

4. _____

see an opera

play golf

5. _____

6. _____

6 Lost tales

A Read the two blog posts. Where did each blogger go? What activity did each one want to do?

NO WAY OUT!

Have you ever visited Mexico? If so, then you know it is famous for its Aztec ruins. Last summer my Spanish class visited Mexico City. We went on a tour of Aztec ruins that are found under the city's main square. We walked for two hours underground in the dark halls. It was like being in a cave. There are many interesting things to see. I wanted to get a better look at a statue, so I went around some ropes that are supposed to keep tourists out. Several minutes later, I came out on the other side, but my group disappeared! I couldn't hear any voices, and I didn't know which way to go. I was too embarrassed to shout, so I wandered around the halls trying to find my group. I started to get nervous. It seemed like I was alone for hours. I walked around in the darkness until I finally heard the professor calling my name. He was very worried, and I was relieved! For the rest of our trip in Mexico, he made sure I never left his sight. My friends still call me "Cave Woman."

NO WAY IN!

I have been to Europe many times but never to Greece until last summer. It was an unforgettable experience! I was staying at a small hotel in Athens. It was in a part of town where most tourists don't stay, but it was cheaper there, and I wanted to practice speaking Greek with people. One evening I went for a walk before dinner. Soon it started to get dark. I didn't want to get lost, and I remembered I had a small map of Athens in my wallet. My wallet! It wasn't in my pocket. I thought, "I've left it in the hotel room . . . and my hotel key is in my wallet!" It took me a long time to get back to the hotel, but I made it. The door was locked, of course. Sometimes I talk to myself when I'm upset. Well, I must have said out loud, "I've lost my wallet, I've locked myself out, and I've missed dinner!" Just then, the hotel manager appeared. I guess he heard me talking. He said something in Greek and pointed to his house. I followed him. He and his family were having a big Greek dinner. They wanted me to join them. The manager eventually let me into my room. But first, I ate one of the best meals I've ever had. And forgetting my wallet was the best mistake I've ever made!

B In which story or stories did the writer(s) do these things? Write *1, 2,* or *1 and 2.*

_____1_____ went to ruins   _____ stayed at a hotel

_____ went to a foreign country   _____ went underground

_____ got lost   _____ made a mistake

_____ got help from someone   _____ went on the trip alone

C Write about an adventure you have had. What happened? What went wrong?

_____

_____

_____

_____

7 Look at the answers. Write questions using *Have you ever . . . ?*

text messaging

rugby match

sushi

Houston

1. **A:** <u>Have you ever sent a text message during class?</u>

   B: No, I've never sent a text message during class.

2. **A:** _____

   B: Actually, I saw a rugby match last week on TV. It was awesome!

3. **A:** _____

   B: Yes, I love sushi.

4. **A:** _____

   B: No, I haven't. But my uncle lives in Houston.

5. **A:** _____

   B: Yes, I visited an amusement park last month.

6. **A:** _____

   B: No, I haven't. I don't think I would like camping.

7. **A:** _____

   B: Yes, I have. I once rode my aunt's motorcycle.

8 Write your own answers to the questions (speaker A) in Exercise 7. Use expressions like the ones from the list.

Yes, I have.	I . . . yesterday.	No, I haven't.	I've never . . .
	I . . . on Monday.		I . . . yet.
	I . . . last year.		
	I . . . in August.		

1. _____

2. _____

3. _____

4. _____

5. _____

6. _____

7. _____

9 **Complete the conversation. Use the simple past or the present perfect of the words given.**

A: _____Have_____ you ever _____lost_____ (lose) anything valuable?

B: Yes, I _____ (lose) my cell phone last month.

A: _____ you _____ (find) it yet?

B: No. Actually, I _____ already _____ (buy) a new one. Look!

A: Oh, that's nice. Where _____ you _____ (buy) it?

B: I _____ (get) it at the mall last weekend. What about you? _____ you ever _____ (lose) anything valuable?

A: Well, I _____ (leave) my leather jacket in a coffee shop a couple of months ago.

B: Oh, no! _____ you _____ (go) back and look for it?

A: Well, I _____ (call) them, but it was gone.

10 **Choose the correct responses.**

1. **A:** Has John visited his brother lately?

   B: _____No, he hasn't._____

   • How many times?
   • No, he hasn't.

2. **A:** Are you having a good time?

   B: _____

   • Yes, in a long time.
   • Yes, really good.

3. **A:** How long did Theresa stay at the party?

   B: _____

   • For two hours.
   • Since midnight.

4. **A:** Have you had breakfast?

   B: _____

   • Yes, in a few minutes.
   • Yes, I've already eaten.

5. **A:** How many times has Tony lost his keys?

   B: _____

   • Twice.
   • Not yet.

6. **A:** Do you want to see that new movie?

   B: _____

   • I never have. What about you?
   • Sure. I hear it's great.

7. **A:** Have you been here long?

   B: _____

   • No, not yet.
   • No, just a few minutes.

8. **A:** Have you seen Sara today?

   B: _____

   • Yes, I saw her this morning.
   • Yes, tomorrow.

11 It's a really nice city.

1 Choose the correct words to complete the sentences.

Singapore

Chicago

1. Prices are high in Singapore. Everything is very ___expensive___ there.
(cheap / expensive / noisy)

2. Chicago has amazing skyscrapers right next to a gorgeous lake. It's a really _____ city.
(beautiful / cheap / quiet)

3. My hometown is not an exciting place. The nightlife there is pretty _____.
(boring / nice / interesting)

4. Some parts of our city are fairly dangerous. It's not very _____ late at night.
(hot / interesting / safe)

5. The streets in this city are always full of people, cars, and buses. It's a very _____ city.
(spacious / crowded / relaxing)

2 Choose the correct questions to complete this conversation.

- ☐ What's the weather like?
- ☐ Is it big?
- ☐ Is the nightlife exciting?
- ☑ What's your hometown like?

A: _What's your hometown like?_

B: My hometown? It's a pretty nice place, and the people are very friendly.

A: _____

B: No, it's fairly small, but it's not too small.

A: _____

B: The winter is wet and really cold. It's very nice in the summer, though.

A: _____

B: No! It's really boring. There are no good restaurants or nightclubs.

3 Choose the correct conjunctions and rewrite the sentences.

> **Grammar note: *And, but, though,* and *however***
>
> **Use *and* for additional information.**
> It's an exciting city, **and** the weather is great.
> **Use *but, though,* and *however* for contrasting information.**
> It's very safe during the day, **but** it's pretty dangerous at night.
> The summers are hot. The evenings are fairly cold, **though**.
> It is a fairly large city. It's not too interesting, **however**.

Colorado

Dubai

Hong Kong

1. Colorado is beautiful in the summer. It's a great place to go hiking. (and / but)

Colorado is beautiful in the summer, and it's a great place to go hiking.

_____

2. Dubai is a very nice place. The summers are terribly hot. (and / though)

_____

_____

3. Hong Kong is an exciting city. It's a fun place to sightsee. (and / however)

_____

_____

4. My hometown has some great restaurants. It's not a good place for shopping. (and / but)

_____

_____

5. Our hometown is somewhat ugly. It has some beautiful old homes. (and / however)

_____

_____

4 Check (✓) if these sentences need *a* or *an*. Then write *a* or *an* in the correct places.

> **Grammar note: A and *an***
>
> Use *a* or *an* with (adverb +) adjective + singular noun.
> It has **a fairly new park**. It's **an old city**.
> Don't use *a* or *an* with (adverb +) adjective.
> It's **fairly new**. It's **old**.

1. ✓ London has *a* very famous Ferris wheel.
2. ☐ Restaurants are very cheap in Ecuador.
3. ☐ Brisbane is clean city.
4. ☐ The buildings in Florence are really beautiful.
5. ☐ Apartments are very expensive in Hong Kong.
6. ☐ Sapporo is very cold city in the winter.
7. ☐ Beijing's museums are really excellent.
8. ☐ Mumbai is exciting place to visit.

5 Complete the description of Paris with *is* or *has*.

PARIS: City of Light

Paris _____ France's biggest city. It _____ a very lively city with an interesting history. It _____ a city of interesting buildings and churches, and it _____ many beautiful parks. It also _____ some of the best museums in the world. Paris _____ nice weather most of the year, but it _____ pretty cold in the winter. It _____ a popular city with foreign tourists and _____ millions of visitors a year. The city _____ famous for its fashion and _____ many excellent stores. Paris _____ convenient trains and buses that cross the city, so it _____ easy for tourists to get around.

6 From city to city

A Scan the webpage. Where is each city?

SEOUL

Seoul was founded in 18 BCE. It is South Korea's capital and today has a population of 10.5 million people. Seoul is famous for producing popular music and films that are very well known in Asia, Latin America, and the Middle East. The city is surrounded by mountains and located on the Han River. It has an excellent transportation system that can take you to 115 museums, monuments, parks, and music festivals throughout the city. The best time to visit Seoul is in the fall and the spring. Winters can be quite cold and summers very hot.

QUITO

Quito sits 2,850 meters above sea level and is the highest capital city in the world. Its population is 2.6 million people. The city is located near the equator in the country of Ecuador (which means "equator" in Spanish). Quito's downtown center, one of the most beautiful in the Americas, has not changed much since the Spanish founded the city in 1534. On a day trip from Quito, you can go walking in the mountains and visit a volcano there. Because of the city's elevation and location on the equator, the weather there is pleasant all year.

RABAT

Rabat is located on the Atlantic Ocean. It was founded in 1146. Although Rabat is the capital of Morocco, its population is only about 580,000 people. The weather is cool at night with hot days in the summer and mild days in the winter. Mawazine, a famous world music festival, takes place in Rabat in the spring. You can visit the Kasbah, an old fortress, and enjoy the architecture, gardens, and the view of the ocean. Rabat's outdoor markets sell beautiful handmade goods. Explore the city and enjoy a delicious Moroccan meal!

B Read the webpage and complete the chart.

City	Date founded	Population	Attractions
Seoul			
Quito			
Rabat			

C Complete the sentences.

1. _____ and _____ have music festivals.
2. _____ is the capital city with the smallest population.
3. _____ is the oldest capital city.
4. _____ has the capital city with the highest altitude.

7 Complete the sentences. Use phrases from the box.

- ☐ shouldn't miss
- ☑ should see
- ☐ can get
- ☐ can take
- ☐ shouldn't stay
- ☐ shouldn't walk

1. You _____should see_____ the new zoo. It's very interesting.

2. You _____ near the airport. It's too noisy.

3. You _____ the museum. It has some new exhibits.

4. You _____ a bus tour of the city if you like.

5. You _____ alone at night. It's too dangerous.

6. You _____ a taxi if you're out late.

8 Complete the conversation with *should* or *shouldn't* and *I* or *you*.

A: I'm taking my vacation in Japan. What _____should I_____ do there?

B: _____ miss Kyoto, the old capital city. There are a lot of beautiful old buildings. For example, _____ see the Ryoanji Temple.

A: Sounds great. Hakone is very popular, too. _____ go there?

B: Yes, _____. It's very interesting, and the hot springs are fantastic.

A: _____ take a lot of money with me?

B: No, _____. You can use the ATMs in Japan.

A: So when _____ go there?

B: In the spring or the fall. You can see the cherry blossoms or the fall colors.

9 **Ask questions about a place you want to visit. Use _can_, _should_, or _shouldn't_.**

1. the time to visit

   What time of year should I visit?

2. things to see and do there

3. things not to do

4. special foods to try

5. fun things to buy

6. other interesting things to do

10 **Rewrite the sentences. Think of another way to express each sentence using the words given.**

1. It's a polluted city.

   It isn't a clean city.   (not clean)

2. You really should visit the new aquarium.

   _____ (not miss)

3. Apartments are not cheap in my country.

   _____ (extremely expensive)

4. This neighborhood is not noisy at all.

   _____ (very quiet)

5. When should we visit the city?

   _____ (a good time)

12 It's important to get rest.

1 Any suggestions?

A Check (✓) the best advice for each health problem.

1. a backache

- ✓ use a heating pad
- ☐ get some exercise
- ☐ drink herbal tea

2. a bad cold

- ☐ see a dentist
- ☐ go to bed and rest
- ☐ go swimming

3. a burn

- ☐ take a multivitamin
- ☐ put it under cold water
- ☐ drink warm milk

4. a headache

- ☐ take some vitamin C
- ☐ take some pain medicine
- ☐ take a cough drop

5. an insect bite

- ☐ apply anti-itch cream
- ☐ use eyedrops
- ☐ drink lots of liquids

6. sore muscles

- ☐ drink lots of hot water
- ☐ take some cold medicine
- ☐ use some ointment

B Write a question about each problem in part A. Then write answers using the words from the box. Use the advice in part A or your own ideas.

> It's important . . .   It's sometimes helpful . . .   It's a good idea . . .

1. A: What should you do for a backache?

   B: It's sometimes helpful to use a heating pad.

2. A: _____

   B: _____

3. A: _____

   B: _____

4. A: _____

   B: _____

5. A: _____

   B: _____

6. A: _____

   B: _____

2 **Rewrite these sentences. Give advice using** *it's important . . . ,* *it's a good idea . . . ,* **or** *it's sometimes helpful . . . .*

Grammar note: Negative infinitives

Problem	Advice	Negative infinitive
For the flu,	don't exercise a lot.	For the flu, it's a good idea **not to exercise** a lot.

1. For a toothache, don't eat cold foods.

   For a toothache, it's important not to eat cold foods.

2. For a sore throat, don't talk too much.

   _____

3. For a burn, don't put ice on it.

   _____

4. For insomnia, don't drink coffee at night.

   _____

5. For a fever, don't get out of bed.

   _____

3 **Check (✓) three health problems you have had. Write what you did for each one. Use the remedies below or your own remedies.**

Health problems

☐ a cough   ☐ a backache

☐ a headache   ☐ the hiccups

☐ insomnia   ☐ a sunburn

☐ a cold   ☐ stress

Some remedies

take some pain medicine

get some medicine from the drugstore

use some lotion

put some ointment on it

take some cough drops

see my doctor/dentist

go to bed

do nothing

Example: *Yesterday, I had a bad headache, so I took some pain medicine.*

1. _____

2. _____

3. _____

4 Learning to laugh

A Scan the article. Check (✓) the sentence that is the better summary of the article.

☐ People who laugh at least once a day live longer than people who don't.
☐ Laughter has important health benefits for your body.

LAUGH IT OFF

Have you laughed today? If so, you probably did a good thing for your health.

Psychologists now consider laughing to be an important practice for good health. Laughter is known to reduce stress, improve the body's ability to fight disease, and make life happier and more interesting. It adds to the pleasure we get from other people and the enjoyment other people get from us.

Dr. Madan Kataria, the founder of Laughter Yoga, discovered that laughter does not have to be real to be good for the body. In Laughter Yoga, people combine yoga breathing with laughter exercises in a group. This allows people to practice laughing without the presence of humor.

Dr. Kataria has found that the body responds well just to the physical act of laughing.

Dr. Annette Goodheart was one of the first doctors in the U.S. to promote laughter for health. In her book *Laughter Therapy: How to Laugh About Everything in Your Life That is Not Really Funny*, she writes, "Everyone usually knows what they think is funny or can laugh at. But I help people laugh about things that aren't funny and support them in re-balancing and resolving their pain."

People who say that laughter is the best medicine might be right. A laugh a day keeps the doctor away!

B Check (✓) True or False.

	True	False
1. Laughter can help the body fight disease.	☐	☐
2. The more you laugh, the more other people like you.	☐	☐
3. Laughter is healthier for you if it is real.	☐	☐
4. Psychologists believe it is healthy to laugh at all situations.	☐	☐
5. Dr. Goodheart helped patients focus only on funny things.	☐	☐

C Describe a time you laughed hard at something. How did you feel afterward?

_____

_____

_____

5 What do you suggest?

A Complete the word map with medicines from the list.

☐ anti-itch cream   ☑ herbal tea   ☐ pain medicine
☐ bandages   ☐ insect spray   ☐ shaving cream
☐ eyedrops   ☐ muscle ointment

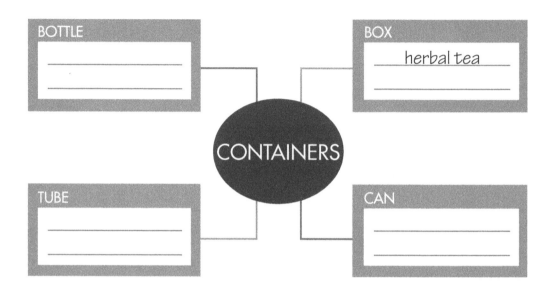

BOTTLE
_____
_____

BOX
__herbal tea__
_____

CONTAINERS

TUBE
_____
_____

CAN
_____
_____

B What should these people buy? Give advice. Use the containers and medicine from part A.

1. Danielle is having trouble sleeping.
   She should buy a box of herbal tea.

2. Simon has a bad headache.
   _____

3. Maria's shoulders are sore after her workout.
   _____

4. There may be mosquitoes where Brenda's camping.
   _____

5. Sam has a cut on his hand.
   _____

6. Graciela has dry, itchy skin on her feet.
   _____

7. Nathan cut his chin when he shaved with soap and water.
   _____

8. Sally's eyes are red and itchy.
   _____

6 **Check (✓) the correct sentences to make conversations.**

1. **Pharmacist:** ☑ Can I help you?

☐ Should I help you?

 Customer: ☐ Yes. Can I have a bottle of pain medicine?

☐ Yes. I suggest a bottle of pain medicine.

Pharmacist: Here you are.

 Customer: ☐ And what do you need for a sunburn?

☐ And what do you have for a sunburn?

Pharmacist: ☐ Do you suggest this lotion?

☐ I suggest this lotion.

 Customer: Thanks.

2. **Pharmacist:** Hi. Can I help you?

 Customer: ☐ Yes. Can I suggest something for sore muscles?

☐ Yes. Could I have something for sore muscles?

Pharmacist: ☐ Sure. Try this ointment.

☐ Sure. Could I try this ointment?

 Customer: ☐ Thanks. And what should you get for the flu?

☐ Thanks. And what do you suggest for the flu?

Pharmacist: ☐ Can I have some of these tablets? They really work.

☐ Try some of these tablets. They really work.

 Customer: ☐ OK, thanks. I'll take them. And you should get a box of tissues.

☐ OK, thanks. I'll take them. And could I have a box of tissues?

Pharmacist: Sure. Here you are.

7 Complete this conversation with the correct words.

A: Wow, you don't look very good! Do you feel OK?

B: No, I think I'm getting a cold. What should I do _____ it?
(for / to / with)

A: You should stay _____ home and go _____ bed.
(at / in / of)   (in / of / to)

B: You're probably right. I've got a really bad cough, too.

A: Try drinking some hot tea _____ honey. It really helps.
(for / of / with)

B: Anything else?

A: Yeah, I suggest you get a big box _____ tissues!
(at / in / of)

8 Give suggestions for these problems. Use words from the box.

| Try . . . | I suggest . . . | You should . . . |

1. I can't stop sneezing.

Try some allergy medicine.

2. I have a stomachache.

_____

3. I don't have any energy.

_____

4. I think I'm getting a cold.

_____

5. I'm stressed out!

_____

6. I have a very sore throat.

_____

13 What would you like?

1 **Show that you agree. Write sentences with the words given.**

1. A: I don't want fast food tonight.

B: _I don't either._ (either)

2. A: I really like Mexican food.

B: _____ (so)

3. A: I'm in the mood for Italian food.

B: _____ (too)

4. A: I can't stand spicy food.

B: _____ (neither)

5. A: I don't like greasy food very much.

B: _____ (either)

6. A: I want to eat healthy food for lunch.

B: _____ (too)

2 | What do you think?

A Look at the pictures. Write sentences about the food. Use the expressions in the box and the given words.

> ### Useful expressions
>
> I love . . .   I'm crazy about . . .
> I can't stand . . .   I'm not crazy about . . .
> I don't like . . . very much.   It's a little too . . .
> I like . . . a lot.

greasy

1. <u>It's a little too greasy.</u>

bland

2. _____

rich

3. _____

salty

4. _____

healthy

5. _____

B What are three of your favorite kinds of food? Write what you like about them.

_____

_____

_____

_____

3 To your taste

A Skim the restaurant reviews. Match the reviewer with the number of stars.

1. Carlota   ★   Awful!

2. Adam   ★ ★ ★   Pretty good.

3. Luka   ★ ★ ★ ★ ★   Fantastic!!

YUM! Restaurant Reviews

Find a restaurant ... 🔍

QUINOA CORNER
175 PLEASANT ST.

Carlota

Quinoa Corner is my latest discovery! This international food restaurant has everything: delicious steak, hamburgers, Mexican enchiladas, Mediterranean salads, and vegetarian and vegan dishes, too. When I was there last Saturday, I ordered a grilled salmon with baby asparagus and a baked potato. Delicious! And the atmosphere is wonderful. The servers are dressed as cowboys and cowgirls. Every hour they do a square dance and sing a song for the diners. I love this place!

Luka

Last Sunday I took my wife to Quinoa Corner. I had sushi with rice and a cucumber salad. My wife had lamb curry with spicy vegetables and garlic bread. For dessert we both had chocolate cake. The sushi was quite good, although the salad was not as fresh as I'd like. My wife said that her curry was delicious, but that the vegetables were a little too salty. And I thought the servers were kind of silly. Despite those problems, we still recommend this restaurant.

Adam

For dinner last Thursday, I visited Quinoa Corner for the first time. I ordered the quinoa burger and an almond milkshake. They served me a real hamburger! While I was trying to explain the mistake to my server, she stepped away and began to dance and sing with the other "cowboys"! It took another half hour before my quinoa burger got to the table. When it did, it was cold, bland, and greasy! I do not recommend this restaurant.

B Read the reviews and complete the chart.

	Carlota	Luka	Luka's wife	Adam
Ordered:				
Problems:	☐ yes ☐ no	☐ yes ☐ no	☐ yes ☐ no	☐ yes ☐ no
Recommends:	☐ yes ☐ no	☐ yes ☐ no	☐ yes ☐ no	☐ yes ☐ no

4 **Check (✓) the item that does not belong in each group.**

1. ☐ apples
☑ broccoli
☐ strawberries

3. ☐ ice cream
☐ iced coffee
☐ iced tea

5. ☐ beef
☐ bread
☐ chicken

2. ☐ sushi
☐ pasta
☐ bread

4. ☐ corn
☐ green beans
☐ pork

6. ☐ a cookie
☐ a turkey sandwich
☐ a hamburger

5 **Use one or more words to complete this conversation between a server and a customer.**

Server: May I take your order?

Customer: _____Yes, I'll have_____ the salmon.

Server: What kind of dressing _____ on your salad – French, blue cheese, or vinaigrette?

Customer: _____ like French, please.

Server: And would you like _____ to drink?

Customer: Yes, _____ have iced coffee.

Server: With milk and sugar?

Customer: Yes, _____.

Server: Anything else?

Customer: No, _____. That'll _____ all.

6 Choose the correct responses.

1. A: What would you like?

    B: <u>I'll have a beef burrito.</u>

- I'll be your server today.
- Yes, I'd like to.
- I'll have a beef burrito.

2. A: Would you like soup or salad?

    B: _____

- I guess I will, thanks.
- I'd like soup, please.
- Yes, please.

3. A: What would you like on your pizza?

    B: _____

- I'll have pepperoni.
- I'd like a soda, please.
- Small, please.

4. A: Would you like anything to drink?

    B: _____

- No, thanks.
- Yes, a hamburger, please.
- I'll have some noodles, please.

5. A: What flavor ice cream would you like?

    B: _____

- Fresh, please.
- Vanilla, please.
- Ice cream, please.

6. A: Would you like anything else?

    B: _____

- Yes, thank you very much.
- Not at all, thanks.
- That'll be all, thanks.

7 Choose the correct words.

1. Baked potatoes are less ____<u>greasy</u>____ than french fries. (greasy / healthy / spicy)

2. In a restaurant, the server takes your _____. (table / order / service)

3. Many people like _____ on their salad. (dessert / dressing / soda)

4. Some people rarely cook with spices. They prefer food to be _____. (bland / hot / rich)

5. Strawberry is a popular ice cream _____. (drink / flavor / meal)

8 Complete the conversation. Use the words and expressions in the box.

- [ ] am
- [ ] can
- [ ] can't stand them
- [ ] do
- [ ] favorite kind of food
- [ ] like it a lot
- [✓] neither
- [ ] so
- [ ] too
- [ ] I'll
- [ ] would

Maria: I feel tired tonight. I really don't want to cook.

Courtney: _____Neither_____ do I. Let's order out. Do you like Chinese food?

Maria: It's delicious! I _____!

Courtney: I do, _____. It's my _____.
Let's call Beijing Express for home delivery.

Maria: Great idea! Their food is always good. I eat there a lot.

Courtney: _____ do I. Well, what _____ you like tonight?

Maria: I'm in the mood for some soup.

Courtney: So _____ I. And I think _____ have orange chicken and fried rice.

Maria: OK, let's order. Oh, wait. They don't take credit cards, and I don't have any cash on me.

Courtney: Neither _____ I. Too bad! What should we do?

Maria: Well, let's look in the refrigerator. Hmm. Do you like boiled eggs?

Courtney: I _____!

Maria: Actually, neither _____ I.

14 It's the coldest city!

1 Geography

A Circle the correct word.

1. This is a mountain with a hole on top. Smoke and lava sometimes come out, and it can be dangerous.
   a. waterfall   **b.** volcano   **c.** hill

2. This is a dry, sandy place. It doesn't rain much here, and there aren't many plants.
   a. desert   **b.** sea   **c.** volcano

3. This is a low area of land between mountains or hills.
   a. island   **b.** valley   **c.** beach

4. This is an area of water with land all around it.
   a. hill   **b.** island   **c.** lake

5. This is a flow of water that happens when a river falls from a high place.
   a. hill   **b.** canyon   **c.** waterfall

6. This is a large area of land that has lots of trees on it.
   a. desert   **b.** forest   **c.** river

B Complete the names. Use words from the box.

☐ Canyon	☐ Falls	☐ Ocean	☑ Lake
☐ Desert	☐ Mount	☐ River	☐ Sea

1. _____Lake_____ Superior
2. Amazon _____
3. Grand _____
4. Atlantic _____
5. Mojave _____
6. Niagara _____
7. Mediterranean _____
8. _____ Everest

2 Write the comparative and superlative forms of the words given.

Spelling note: Comparatives and superlatives	Adjective	Comparative	Superlative
Add **-er** or **-est** to most words.	long	long**er**	the long**est**
Add **-r** or **-st** to words ending in **-e**.	large	larg**er**	the larg**est**
Drop the y and add **-ier** or **-iest**.	dry	dr**ier**	the dr**iest**
Double the final consonant and add **-er** or **-est**.	big	bi**gger**	the bi**ggest**

1. busy   _busier_   _the busiest_

2. cool   _____ _____

3. friendly   _____ _____

4. heavy   _____ _____

5. nice   _____ _____

6. noisy   _____ _____

7. old   _____ _____

8. safe   _____ _____

9. small   _____ _____

10. wet   _____ _____

3 Complete this conversation. Use the superlative form of the words given.

Keegan: So where did you go for your vacation, Kathy?

Kathy: Japan.

Keegan: How exciting! Did you have a good time?

Kathy: It was terrific! I think Japan is ____the most exciting____ (exciting) country in Asia.

Keegan: Well, it certainly has some of _____ (interesting) cities in the world – Tokyo, Osaka, and Kyoto.

Kathy: Yeah. I had _____ (good) time in Kyoto. It's _____ (beautiful) city I've ever seen. Of course, it's also one of _____ (popular) tourist attractions. It was _____ (crowded) city I visited this summer.

Keegan: I've always wanted to visit Japan. What's it like in the winter?

Kathy: Actually, I think that's _____ (bad) time to visit because I don't like cold weather. However, I think the Sapporo Snow Festival is _____ (fascinating) festival in the world.

4 Complete these sentences. Use the comparative or the superlative form of the words given.

Badwater Basin

the Suez Canal

Mount Waialeale

1. Badwater Basin in California's Death Valley is _____*the lowest*_____ (low) point in North America.

2. The Suez Canal joins the Mediterranean and Red Seas. It is 190 kilometers (118 miles) long. It is _____*longer than*_____ (long) the Panama Canal.

3. Mount Waialeale in Hawaii gets 1,170 centimeters (460 inches) of rain a year. It is _____ (wet) place on Earth!

4. Canada and Russia are _____ (large) countries in the world.

5. Russia is _____ (large) Canada.

6. _____ (high) waterfall in the world is in Venezuela.

7. The Atacama Desert in Chile is _____ (dry) place in the world.

8. _____ (hot) capital city in the world is Muscat, Oman.

9. The continent of Antarctica is _____ (cold) any other place in the world.

10. The Himalayas are some of _____ (dangerous) mountains to climb.

11. Mont Blanc in the French Alps is _____ (high) the Matterhorn in the Swiss Alps.

12. The Pacific Ocean is _____ (deep) the Atlantic Ocean. At one place, the Pacific Ocean is 11,033 meters (36,198 feet) deep.

5 The coldest and the windiest!

A Scan the article about Antarctica. In what ways is it different from other places on Earth? Why do scientists work there?

ANTARCTICA is the most southern continent in the world. It's like nowhere else on Earth. It's much larger than Europe and nearly twice the size of Australia. It's an icy plateau with the South Pole at its center. Antarctica is the coldest and windiest place in the world, even colder and windier than the North Pole. Although 98 percent of Antarctica is covered in ice, it is considered a desert. Along the coast, annual precipitation is only 200 millimeters (eight inches) a year. Very few plants grow there, but there is some wildlife, including whales, seals, and penguins. In the summer, the sun shines for 24 hours a day, but in the winter, it's completely dark for about three months.

When Captain James Cook sailed around the continent in the 1770s, he found no one living there. Today, a few scientists work in Antarctica, but they only spend fairly short periods of time there. Many of these scientists live and work on the Antarctic Peninsula. This area is the closest part of Antarctica to South America, the continent's nearest neighbor. Many of these scientists are studying the effects of climate change there. Antarctica has warmed by about 2.5 degrees Celsius since 1950. Some ice is melting in certain parts of the continent. However, unlike the vast melting that is happening in the Arctic, the ice in Antarctica is actually growing in spite of global warming.

Scientists think that this cold and lonely place can teach us a lot about the earth and how to keep it safe.

B Read about Antarctica. Check (✓) True or False.

	True	False
1. Antarctica is bigger than Europe.	☐	☐
2. The North Pole is the coldest place in the world.	☐	☐
3. The coasts in Antarctica get a lot of snow.	☐	☐
4. In Antarctica, it never gets dark in the summer.	☐	☐
5. Captain Cook discovered a few people living in Antarctica.	☐	☐
6. The Antarctic Peninsula is the closest part of Antarctica to South America.	☐	☐
7. Ice in Antarctica is melting throughout the continent.	☐	☐

6 Geography quiz

Use the words in the box. Write questions about the pictures. Then circle the correct answers.

☐ How big   ☐ How deep   ☐ How long
☐ How cold   ☐ How far   ☑ How high

Angel Falls

1. <u>How high is Angel Falls?</u>
   a. It's 979 meters (3,212 feet) tall.
   (b.) It's 979 meters high.

2. _____
   a. It's 6,300 kilometers (3,917 miles) long.
   b. It's 6,300 kilometers high.

the Yangtze River

Antarctica

3. _____
   a. It gets up to –88.3 degrees Celsius (–126.9 degrees Fahrenheit).
   b. It gets down to –88.3 degrees Celsius.

4. _____
   a. It's about 2,000 kilometers (1,200 miles).
   b. It's about 2,000 square kilometers.

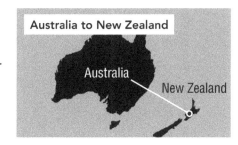

Australia to New Zealand

Australia

New Zealand

the Amazon Rain Forest

5. _____
   a. It's 6 million square kilometers (2.5 million square miles).
   b. It's 6 million kilometers long.

6. _____
   a. It's about 1.6 kilometers (1 mile) big.
   b. It's about 1.6 kilometers deep.

the Grand Canyon

7 **Answer these questions about your country.**

1. How big is the largest city?

_____

2. What's the wettest month?

_____

3. What's the driest month?

_____

4. How hot does it get in the summer?

_____

5. How cold does it get in the winter?

_____

6. How high is the highest mountain?

_____

7. What's the most beautiful town to visit?

_____

8 **Match the words with their opposites.**

1. biggest _f_	**a.** better
2. bad _____	**b.** wettest
3. shorter _____	**c.** colder
4. worse _____	**d.** drier
5. worst _____	**e.** hottest
6. near _____	**f.** smallest
7. lowest _____	**g.** far
8. driest _____	**h.** bigger
9. hot _____	**i.** good
10. shortest _____	**j.** best
11. hotter _____	**k.** low
12. smaller _____	**l.** highest
13. coldest _____	**m.** longest
14. wetter _____	**n.** wet
15. dry _____	**o.** taller
16. high _____	**p.** cold

15 What are you doing later?

1 Match the words in columns A and B. Write the names of the events.

A	B	
☑ baseball	☐ appointment	**1.** *baseball game*
☐ birthday	☐ concert	**2.**
☐ car	☑ game	**3.**
☐ class	☐ match	**4.**
☐ medical	☐ party	**5.**
☐ rock	☐ race	**6.**
☐ tennis	☐ reunion	**7.**

2 Read Joe's calendar and write about his plans each day. Use be going to.

	Calendar					
	Day Week Month Year					🔍
March						< This week >
Sunday	Monday	Tuesday	Wednesday	Thursday	Friday	Saturday
4	5	6	7	8	9	10
afternoon – play tennis with Brock	attend the managers' meeting at work	6:00 p.m. – see a movie with Angela	night – watch the soccer match with Annie and Bob	noon – have lunch with Paco	evening – go to the rock concert with friends	stay home and do laundry

1. On Sunday afternoon, Joe is going to play tennis with Brock.

2. _____

3. _____

4. _____

5. _____

6. _____

7. _____

3 Complete this conversation. Use *be going to* and the verbs given.

Stacey: What _____are_____ you _____going to do_____ this weekend, Hannah? (do)

Hannah: I _____ to a jazz concert on Saturday. (go)

Stacey: That sounds interesting.

Hannah: Yeah. There's a free concert in the park. What about you, Stacey?

Stacey: Well, Ryan and I _____ a baseball game in the afternoon. (see)

Hannah: And what _____ you _____ in the evening? (do)

Stacey: Ryan _____ his mother in the hospital. (visit) But I _____ not _____ anything really. (do)

Hannah: Well, I _____ some friends over for a barbecue. (have) Would you like to come?

Stacey: Thanks, I'd love to!

4 Choose the correct responses.

1. **A:** There's a basketball game on TV tonight. Do you want to watch it?

   B: __I'm sorry. I'm working late tonight.__

   • How about this evening?

   • I'm sorry. I'm working late tonight.

   • Yes, it does.

2. **A:** Would you like to have dinner at Bella's Bistro tonight?

   B: _____

   • No, I'm not doing anything.

   • Sorry, I'm going away next week.

   • Yes, that sounds great! But it's my turn to pay.

3. **A:** Do you want to go hiking tomorrow?

   B: _____

   • Yes, I'm going to.

   • Can we go to a late show?

   • Sure, I'd love to.

4. **A:** How about going to a movie on Saturday?

   B: _____

   • Oh, I'm sorry. I can't.

   • Nothing special.

   • No, I wouldn't.

5 Write invitations to this week's events in Eagleton.

Exciting things to do this week in EAGLETON!

MONDAY	TUESDAY	WEDNESDAY	THURSDAY
Pop concert Ellie Goulding	**Summer Festival** Lots to do for everyone!	**Musical** Jersey Boys	**Museum** Modern art exhibition opening

1. *Are you doing anything on Monday evening? Do you want to see a pop concert?* OR
   I'm going to go to the Ellie Goulding concert on Monday. Would you like to come?

2. _____

3. _____

4. _____

6 Write about how often you do these leisure activities. Use the expressions in the box.

I . . . almost every weekend.
I never . . .
I often . . .
I sometimes . . . in the summer.
I . . . three or four times a year.

1. _____

2. _____

3. _____

4. _____

5. _____

6. _____

1 go to the park

2 go to concerts

3 have parties at home

4 see plays

5 watch horror movies

6 go on picnics

7 I need help!

A Read Hannah's social media post and the comments from her friends. Why does she need help?

Wall | Find friends | Chat Profile | Sign out

Hannah 1h ago

Guess what? I'm moving! Is anyone around Saturday morning and (maybe?) afternoon to help me move things to my new apartment? I only have a few heavy things, but I could use all the help I can get. I'll provide pizza for dinner! Tell your friends and let me know!

Pablo 58 minutes ago

Cool, where are you moving? I wish I could help you Saturday, but I'm going to the beach. Don't hate me. I'm available on Sunday . . . but that probably doesn't help you. Sorry!

Richard 55 minutes ago

Congratulations on the new place! I can help, but not until the afternoon. My study group is getting together to prepare for the chemistry exam on Monday (yikes!). See you after lunch?

Lien 50 minutes ago

Whoo-hoo, new apartment! Saturday morning I have to go to my little brother's baseball tournament. But I'll come over right after it's finished. What's the address?

Kalil 42 minutes ago

I'm so sorry, Hannah. I'm going to be working all weekend. I know, bummer. Can't wait to visit, though. Save me a slice of pizza! I like leftovers. ;-)

Rachel 30 minutes ago

I can't wait to see your new apartment! I'm going to visit my grandmother all day, so unfortunately I can't come until the evening – probably when the pizza arrives! Hope that's OK . . .

Eliana 24 minutes ago

Oh, bad timing! I have the city bicycle race on Saturday morning. But I can come when it's over. In fact, I'm going to keep riding past the finish line and straight to your place! See you in the afternoon.

Daichi 15 minutes ago

Pizza?! I'm in. But wait. I need to drive my sister to her dance class and then to her basketball game. Argh. Can she move in with you? Just kidding. I'll be there by 3:00.

B Match Hannah's friends with their reasons for not being able to help her or for showing up to help late.

1. _____ has a bicycle race.
2. _____ has to study.
3. _____ has to drive his sister around.
4. _____ is going to the beach.
5. _____ is going to work all weekend.
6. _____ is going to a baseball tournament.
7. _____ is going to visit her grandmother.

   a. Daichi
   b. Eliana
   c. Kalil
   d. Pablo
   e. Rachel
   f. Richard
   g. Lien

8 **Read these messages. What did the caller say? Write the messages another way using _tell_ or _ask_.**

For: _Mr. Jones_

Message: _The meeting is at 10:30. Arrive 10 minutes early._

1. Please tell Mr. Jones that the meeting is at 10:30.

Could you ask him to arrive 10 minutes early?

For: _Ms. Rodriguez_

Message: _We need the report by noon. Call Ms. Brady as soon as possible._

2. _____

_____

For: Mr. Welch

Message: The new laptop is ready. Pick it up this afternoon.

3. _____

_____

9 **Look at the text messages. Write sentences asking someone to give these messages.**

Grammar note: Negative infinitives	
Request	**Message**
Don't call him today.	Please ask Jan **not to call** him today.
Don't go home yet.	Could you tell him **not to go** home yet?

60% 🔋

< Back　　　　　Alan　　　　　☰

Hi Michael. Don't come to the airport until midnight. The plane is going to be late.

1. _____

_____

_____

60% 🔋

< Back　　　　　Sierra　　　　　☰

Hey Lucy. We're meeting at Pete's house before the concert. Don't forget the tickets.

2. _____

_____

_____

60% 🔋

< Back　　　　　Marta　　　　　☰

Chris! The surprise party starts at noon. Don't be late!

3. _____

_____

_____

10 Choose the correct words.

Receptionist: Hello. McKenzie Corporation.

Mr. Brown: _____May I_____ speak to Mr. Scott Myers, please?
(May I / Would you)

Receptionist: I'm _____. He's not in. _____ a message?
(busy / sorry)   (Can I leave / Can I take)

Mr. Brown: Yes, please. This is Mr. Brown. _____ you _____
(Would / Please)   (tell him that / ask him to)

I have to reschedule our meeting? My phone number is 303-555-9001.

_____ you _____?
(Please / Could)   (ask him to call me / ask me to call him)

Receptionist: OK, Mr. Brown. I'll _____ the message.
(give him / tell him)

Mr. Brown: Thank you very much. Good-bye.

11 Match the questions with the correct responses.

☐ Let me see if she's in.	☑ That's OK. I'll call back.
☐ This is John. John Abrams.	☐ Sure, I'd love to come. Thanks.
☐ Oh, no. I don't eat meat.	☐ Yes. My number is 303-555-3241.

1. I'm sorry. She's busy at the moment.
That's OK. I'll call back.

2. Could I ask her to call you back?
_____

3. Who's calling, please?
_____

4. Would you like to come to a party?
_____

5. Could I speak to Tiffany, please?
_____

6. Why don't we eat at Sam's Steakhouse tonight?
_____

16 How have you changed?

1 Choose the correct responses.

1. A: Hey, you really look different.

   B: _Well, I've grown a mustache._

- I moved into a new house.
- I'm more outgoing than before.
- Well, I've grown a mustache.

2. A: I haven't seen you for ages.

   B: _____

- I know. How have you been?
- Well, I got a bank loan.
- My new job is more stressful.

3. A: You know, I have three kids now.

   B: _____

- No, I haven't graduated from college yet.
- Wow, I can't believe it!
- Say, you've really changed your hair.

4. A: How are you?

   B: _____

- I hope to get my driver's license soon.
- Well, actually, I turned 18.
- I'm doing really well.

2 Complete the sentences. Use information in the box and the present perfect.

  ☐ fall in love   ☐ get two pay raises   ☐ start an online course

1. JoAnn _____ this year. Now she has enough
money to buy a house.

2. Irvin _____. He's studying to become a
graphic designer.

3. Gisela and Russ _____. They're going to get
married in December.

3 Describe how these people have changed. Use the present or the past tense.

Before

Now

1. Mr. and Mrs. Kim <u>had a baby</u>.

Before

Now

2. Sara _____.

Before

Now

3. Ella _____.

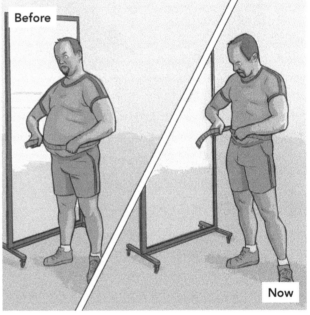

Before

Now

4. Ron _____.

4 Rewrite these sentences. Find another way to say each sentence using the words given.

1. I've grown out my hair.

  <u>My hair is longer now.</u> (longer)

2. Raquel gained a lot of weight.

  _____ (heavier)

3. Ben goes to a new school now.

  _____ (change)

4. Helen and George got divorced last year.

  _____ (married)

5. Traci quit eating fast food.

  _____ (healthier)

6. We quit working out at the gym.

  _____ (not go)

5 Life changes

A Read the passages on the left in part B. Complete these sentences.

1. _____ had an interesting job two years ago.

2. _____ had money problems two years ago.

3. _____ was a student two years ago.

B Now read the passages on the right. Match the people's lives two years ago with their lives now.

Rafael

Diane and her husband

Krystina

Two years ago	Now
1. Rafael Two years ago, I was a student, and I thought life was really good. I got up late. I spent the day talking to friends, and then I studied all night. I wore jeans and sweatshirts and had long hair and a beard. I felt free. _____	**a.** Now my life has completely changed. I got married six months ago! My husband and I often have friends over for dinner. We're taking classes several nights a week. It's great! We're even talking about starting a family soon.
2. Diane I moved to a new town two years ago. My job was interesting, but I was single and I didn't have any friends. People at work were friendly but not very outgoing. We never did anything after work. _____	**b.** Now I work as a computer programmer for an international company. I've moved to Seoul and have started to learn Korean. Korean food is great, and I've gained a few pounds. I feel much happier and healthier.
3. Krystina My life seemed to come to an end two years ago. I lost my job. Then I lost weight and looked terrible. Money became a problem. I was very sad. I needed some good luck. _____	**c.** Now I actually look forward to getting up early in the morning and going to work. Of course, I dress up now, and my hair is shorter. But I don't really mind. At least my evenings are free!

C Underline at least two changes in each person's life.

6 Complete the sentences. Use the words in the box.

☐ broke	☐ graduation	☐ responsibilities
☐ career	☑ loan	☐ successful

1. Rhonda wants to pay off her student ____loan____ before she buys a car.

2. I'd like to be _____ in my first job. Then I can get a better job and a raise.

3. I go to school, and I have a family and a part-time job. I have a lot of _____.

4. After _____, Amelia and Lee plan to look for jobs.

5. Max lost his job. Now he's _____, and he can't pay his rent.

6. What _____ are you most interested in pursuing?

7 Complete this conversation. Use the words given.

Mariko: What ____do you plan to do____ (plan, do) this summer, Brian?

Brian: I _____ (want, get) a summer job.
I _____ (like, save) money for a vacation.

Mariko: Really? Where _____ (like, go)?

Brian: I _____ (love, travel) to Latin America.
What about you, Mariko?

Mariko: Well, I _____ (not go, get) a job right away. First, I _____ (want, go) to Spain and Portugal.

Brian: Sounds great, but how _____ (go, pay) for it?

Mariko: I _____ (hope, borrow) some money from my brother. I have a good excuse. I _____ (plan, take) courses in Spanish and Portuguese.

Brian: Oh, I'm tired of studying!

Mariko: I love to study. I also _____ (hope, take) people on tours to Latin America. Why don't you come on my first tour?

Brian: Count me in!

8 **Imagine you have these problems. Write three sentences about changing your situation. Use the words in the box.**

1. I just moved to a new town, and I don't know anyone. I never do anything after work. People at work don't really talk to me. I haven't had a date in about four months. And I never find anything fun to do on the weekends.

> I'm going to . . .   I want to . . .   I plan to . . .

_____
_____
_____
_____

2. I've become less careful about my health lately. I've stopped jogging because I'm bored with it. I've started eating more fast food because I'm too tired to cook after work. And I can't sleep at night.

> I'm going to . . .   I'd like to . . .   I'd love to . . .

_____
_____
_____
_____
_____

3. My job is so boring. I spend two hours driving to and from work every day, and I don't make enough money! I can't find a new job, though, because of my poor computer skills.

> I hope to . . .   I want to . . .   I plan to . . .

_____
_____
_____
_____

9 **Choose the correct words to complete each sentence. Use the correct form of the word and add any words if necessary.**

1. Floyd hopes to _____<u>move</u>_____ to a small town.
   (move / live / change)

2. This job is _____ my last job.
   (outgoing / stressful / crowded)

3. After graduation, Kira plans _____ for an international company.
   (play / work / move)

4. Stephanie's salary is much _____ before. She had to take a pay cut.
   (low / short / high)

5. I hope to buy a house soon. I need _____ a bank loan.
   (open / start / get)

6. Neil and Kelly got _____ last summer. The wedding will be in April.
   (engage / marry)

10 **Advise people how to make changes in their lives. Use expressions like the ones in the box.**

> Why don't you . . .   You should . . .   You shouldn't . . .

1. I've gained a lot of weight this year.
   _____

2. My hair is longer, but it doesn't look good.
   _____

3. I've gotten tired of wearing the same old clothes.
   _____

4. I want to start a successful business.
   _____

5. I'm often bored on weekends.
   _____

6. I don't really have any goals.
   _____

7. I've finished this textbook, but I still want to improve my English!
   _____